griefbeing

Nicole Callihan

LILY POETRY REVIEW BOOKS

Published by Lily Poetry Review Books
223 Winter Street
Whitman, MA 02382

https://lilypoetryreview.blog/

ISBN: 978-1-957755-56-4

Library of Congress Control Number: 2025933226

Cover design by Martha McCollough

griefbeing...

grief being its own sort of desire

you should hear the gulls this morning

my horoscope tells me to stop pretending

everything is okay   but isn't it?

light on water   blah blah blah

and the crabbers catching crabs

and the sails still furled

an older couple rows into shore

geese lift into the broken sky

their wings more shadow than reflection

grief being somewhat symmetrical

my grandfather could balance a spoon on his nose

or was that my father?

here is a bladder of warm water to ease your pain

here is a table improperly set

for a period of my youth my mother could not bear to look at me

I had bad hair

instead of sitting across from her at the table

she asked me to sit beside her

that way you won't turn my stomach, she said

for a long time I believed this was a funny story

grief being made of mesh

as might be seen at the aviary,
to keep the birds in

or like when Zoë baked me a cake,
to keep the bugs away

or in the Russian net of a bridal veil,
to symbolize modesty & obedience

also, after a fire, in grafting,
when donor skin is unavailable

grief being spade and hoe

of furrow and matter   bonemeal
hormone   sweet mulch   swale
and tilth   the grey ring in the sink
after sudsing   of frost date
of unamended soil balled & burlapped
a one-wheeled barrel filled w/ heads
of yesterday's hydrangeas   o tender
bareroot   I ache for you

grief being a little like a spoon

knocking against a bowl

grief being a pink pearl

a mixture of an abrasive and rubber
vulcanized to bond the ingredients
carried in a star-strewn satchel
knocking against the knee of the girl
her graphite mistakes to be rubbed
so hard as to make a hole in the paper
in her chest in the schoolroom's light

grief being an ad at the laundromat

the way you hold the warm towels

or like how if it's raining you say, *see, rain*

or if it's sunny, you say, *see, sun*

a man dries his face with a clean shirt

a woman matches her 10,000th pair of socks

both events go uncelebrated

no one is counting

grief being a moveable city

in such that Chinatown is uptown
that the Soho corner where you smoked
in the snow is deep in Sunnyside
in the even deeper summer and the flowers
you threw at the feet of the angels
in Harlem   their petals are crushed
in Brighton where an old man sings
under a Morningside moon

grief being a swatch of blue

a rectangle in an unborn son's room

morning glory   secret cove   sleepy hollow

o snowdrop   balmy   respite   open seas

loyal   stream   that little dump truck

undumped   vast sky   rarified air

the cosmos in the can so different

than the cosmos on the wall   so

different than the cosmos where

you began   glimmer in my eye

stardew turned atmospheric splinter

grief being of "language"

or, what my students call *"a tool"*
A tool? I w/ chisel say
w/ screwdriver w/ hammer
w/ clamp wrench axe & drill
in what task have you been aided
in accomplishing I ask
my god rusts in a metal box
hangs from a stranger's belt
sky as mere container for heaven
the half-life of the living

grief being a pitched tent

when autumn coming came
the ball jars on the wooden table
held nasturtiums and wine
a stone in the throat   how
shameful to be alive and wade
into a cold lake under the sky

grief being thin as an envelope

flat

so flat

& verily fragile

beloved item of the archivist

the veins visible through the skin

the hand which shook while writing the words

the dried-out inkwell   the birds

the flag raised to surrender

o who can I tell

o dear

dear

grief being rather equine

of hide, hair, milk, meat
the thing one rides in on

the thing on which one departs
of flies in your eyes

this twitching at this hour
in this time in this field

grief being such a drag

what the cat leaves at your feet, or;
the widower in the wee hours
staring into the milky mirror
his wife's billowy blouse
the elastic of her underpants
smear of her lipstick on his mouth
he falls to his knees
reaches for the face before him

grief being yet another sunrise

you don't have to sleep
I mean, eventually you do
your body will shut down
oranges can help/ fresh air
still the planet on its axis
take a sweater to the sea
it will not be cold   it will be
so dark you believe it is cold
bring bread for the birds

grief being that song from childhood

o spider o rollerskates
o jesus o jesus o jesus
how my knees used to bruise
the pears   the sky
I am so blue and purply
even your thumb hurts me

grief being a procession of people

usually organized along a street,
often in costume, often accompanied
by marching bands, floats,
hats, flowers, baton twirlers,
sometimes very large balloons,
like this one, in which I see your face,
the whole parade of your body

grief being and also not being

the onions translucent in the pan
mother's silk nighty   in the dark house
I move from room to room
my *things* surround me
the spoon on my grandfather's nose
my father w/ his teeth in his hand
the name I call myself—*I, I, I,*
I say—as if in calling I return

Acknowledgments

Grateful acknowledgment to the editors of the following magazines where some of these poems first appeared or are forthcoming:

Fledgling Rag: Desire, Mesh, Equine

The Kenyon Review: Procession of People, Pink Pearl, Moveable City, & Envelope

The Leavings Lit Mag: Symmetrical

Plume: Swatch of Blue, Pitched Tent, Childhood Song

About the Author

Winner of the Alma Award, Nicole Callihan's *SLIP* was published by Saturnalia in March 2025. Her book, *chigger ridge,* was selected by Sandra Lim to receive The Tenth Gate Prize (The Word Works 2024). Other books include *This Strange Garment* (Terrapin 2023) and the 2019 novella, *The Couples.* Her work has appeared in *The Kenyon Review, Copper Nickel, Tin House, Conduit, The American Poetry Review,* and as a Poem-a-Day selection from the Academy of American Poets. Find out more at www.nicolecallihan.com.

www.ingramcontent.com/pod-product-compliance
Lightning Source LLC
Chambersburg PA
CBHW081726120626
46550CB00010B/3270